To Nina
With l

The Pocket Book of Laughter

WAYS TO LAUGH AND PLAY
MORE IN EVERYDAY LIFE

Lisa Sturge

The Pocket Book of Laughter
Ways to laugh and play more in everyday life
by Lisa Sturge
Copyright © 2013 by Lisa Sturge.
All rights reserved.

Published by Laughterlines Coaching

Layout and Cover Design by Marian Way

Cartoon Illustrations by Simon Chadwick
www.ceratopia.co.uk

The author asserts the moral right to be identified as the author of this work.

ISBN: 978-1-291-38002-6

For Ed, Isaac and Ollie

Acknowledgements

My grateful thanks go to Dr Madan Kataria and the Chichester Laughter Club.

Heaps of gratitude also go to Marian Way, Kate Beaumont, Daphne Spalton, Janine Howe, Helen Connelly, Tom Ambrose, Julie Whitehead and to all my wonderful family and friends who have encouraged me along the way.

Foreword

The world needs more laughter.

Laughing with others brings a special connection, a universal understanding and encourages peace. This Pocket Book of Laughter aims to encourage people of all ages to laugh joyfully together and to celebrate daily life.

Life is not always easy, yet we can focus our attention on loving and laughing not just because it feels wonderful and is good for our mind, body and spirit, but because when we do so we are reminded of the pure joy of Being.

This pocket book is a handy and portable reference bank of ideas for more laughter. It suggests a variety of ways in which we can have more fun and playfulness every day. It encourages us to actively choose our own entertainment rather than relying on others to amuse us. Through laughter and playfulness we can learn from each other, share our happiness and communicate without the need for words.

The vision of the laughter movement is World Peace through laughter. This book is a timely reminder that the way forward does not always have to be serious and that playfulness is central to our health and well-being.

Read, laugh and enjoy!

Dr Madan Kataria,
Founder of the Worldwide Laughter Yoga Movement

*If you laugh you change;
and when you change – the
world changes.*

- Dr Madan Kataria

Why Laugh?

Some of the many benefits of laughter

✴ Laughing can strengthen the immune system, release tension in the body and promote relaxation.

✴ Laughing can bond relationships, increase confidence and unite communities.

✴ Laughter reminds people of all the things they have in common.

★ Laughing helps groups to connect joyfully and meaningfully regardless of age, gender, race or religion.

★ Laughing brings a glow to the cheeks, a twinkle to the eyes and lightness to the day.

★ Laughter is the universal language and the icing on the fruit cake of life.

Laughter illuminates life and nourishes the soul.

So how do we encourage more everyday laughter?

Jokes and humour

Many of us watch comedy shows, visit comedy clubs or listen to comedy programmes on the radio and internet. Some of these are superb and a source of much hilarity and amusement. However, one of the drawbacks with relying solely on external influences to stimulate our laughter is that, in between the funny shows and jokes, laughter can easily be forgotten.

Learning from the experts

The experts on laughter are children. Children can laugh up to 400 times a day on average compared to most adults, who laugh generally only a mere 15 times a day. Children do not rely on jokes or comedy sketches for their laughter; they access this innate skill naturally by simply being playful.

Playfulness

Anyone can start by becoming more playful, regardless of age. Play is essential for optimum physical and mental well being, work and socialising. Playing refreshes body and mind, strengthens imagination and can be the source of inspiration for many. In today's often frenetic world, being playful provides an important opportunity to learn, explore and relax.

Now for some frivolous, fun, FREE ways to introduce more playfulness, smiles and laughter into everyday life...

Start gently ...

Give yourself permission.

Often it may feel like you cannot smile or laugh because of external circumstances, but you can choose to be open to happiness whenever you want. There may never be a perfect time for laughter, so be ready to laugh at any time.

Be willing.

Be willing to smile and be willing to laugh. Loosen your body, shake out, move around, stretch and imagine connecting with the mischievous, playful side of you.

Start with a smile.

On tricky or challenging days if you can't laugh or do not want to, then be kind to yourself and smile. Smiling for more than 30 seconds releases endorphins and boosts the immune system. Waking up with a gentle smile signals a loving intention for the day.

Pull faces.

Warm up your face in a playful manner. Pull faces as if you were very young and find out how many different faces you can pull without using your hands. Ask a friend or colleague which one is the funniest and try it out during the day at regular intervals.

Eyebrow dancing.

Put on some groovy music and let your eyebrows go berserk in time to the rhythm. This is best done with another person so you can see each other's faces. Think of them as caterpillars doing 'the twist'.

Practise laughter sounds.

Play with different laughter sounds:
ho ho, hu hu, ha ha, hoo hoo,
hee hee. Experiment with pitch,
volume, tone and length of laugh.
Although the brain can tell the
difference between a real laugh
and a pretend one, your body
doesn't care! Your body will start
to release endorphins as you try
out the laughter sounds and if you
are willing and playful, then real
laughter will emerge.

Teach others the laughter sounds.

There is a deep 'ho' in the belly, a 'hu' just under the ribcage, the 'ha' comes from the heart, the 'hoo' from the throat and the 'hee' from the head. You may discover one or two of your own! Place a hand at each area when you laugh to feel the vibrations. Experiment with the different sounds.

Gradual chuckle.

Slowly start to move your toes and chuckle gently, then wiggle your torso and laugh more as the laughter moves up your body. Let it become as loud and as free as it likes.

Get to know your playful side.

We all have a playful, cheeky side of us that is very childlike. Imagine what this part could look like if it was a person or cartoon figure. Picture the clothes he or she would wear and what his or her voice would sound like. Conjure up this cheeky figure whenever you need a bit of light relief or you are having trouble letting go of seriousness.

Extend your comfort zone.

Try a new hobby and step out of your everyday routine to experience something new just once to see how you feel. New activities often lead to loads of laughter, especially if you involve a friend in your new endeavours. You can both giggle at your first clumsy attempts to ice a cake, abseil or tune your car engine, and as you get better you can laugh at all the memories.

Go at your own pace.

Laughter is not a competition; your laughter is as unique as your fingerprints. Do what feels right for you and explore your *own* laughter at your *own* pace.

Verbal fun ...

Silly voices.

Practise explaining and conversing in strange and unfamiliar voices. Experiment with slow drawls, pitch and volume. Talk to your family in a Darth Vader voice or order coffee in your poshest accent.

Tell an outrageous lie.

The more ridiculous the better. Sometimes life is a bit mundane so have fun with creating imaginary, inventive scenarios that make you and other people smile.

Cartoon voices.

Talk for 5 minutes like Donald Duck, Mickey Mouse or Shrek, while keeping your face really serious.

Talk gibberish.

When least expected, slip into complete nonsense language to argue your case or discuss something in detail. Use ridiculous sounds, gestures and noises to make it as funny as possible to do. This strategy can be very useful for talking with teenagers. They may not understand, but you will be able to vent your frustrations together and hopefully everyone will end up laughing.

Embarrassing moments.

Start a meeting off with 'mistakes I have made' or 'confessions of embarrassment'. These can be bravely shared amongst the whole team or quietly confided to a fellow trusted colleague. Reminiscing about embarrassing incidents is guaranteed to encourage smiles or chuckles. Learning to laugh at yourself frees you to take risks and extend your boundaries.

Laughter quotes.

Find laughter quotes or sayings that remind you to laugh. For example, *"We don't laugh because we're happy, we're happy because we laugh"* – William James. Create a bookmark with your favourite one or make one into a screen saver for your computer.

Talk about laughter.

Talk to others about what makes them laugh. Asking others what has happened recently to make them giggle is a sure way of encouraging laughter to flow.

Funny thoughts.

Think a funny thought or conjure up a vivid memory about a hilarious incident that did happen or could have happened. Now exaggerate it even further… this may help you smile or chuckle whenever you need to.

Tongue twisters.

Exchange tongue twisters. Do you remember "She sells sea shells on the sea shore"? Invent your own, about yourself or everyday situations in your life.

Clever captions.

Collect a range of different photos
or pictures of comical events.
Pin these up on a wall and invite
people to add captions or speech
bubbles.

News bulletin.

When faced with a tricky moment or situation, pretend you are the newsreader who has stumbled on this latest story. You have to report on it in flamboyant, dramatic or snooty style, exaggerating the drama for media purposes.

Word of the week.

Take turns choosing a fun and ridiculous word for the week. See who in your home or office can get the daft word into everyday conversations during the week. Display the word boldly and brightly to remind everyone of the challenge. Great for making cold calling fun or for challenging your family at the dinner table.

Fantasy journey.

On the way to work or the shops, create an imaginary story in your mind so that you can relay it to someone when you get there. This will make the journey more fun and they can laugh at the idea of you snogging George Clooney on the number 12 bus or being mistaken for Wonder Woman. Great way of exercising your creative muscles.

No teeth conversation.

Have a serious chat with a friend
without showing any of your teeth
at all and see what happens.

Inventing limericks.

Make up some fun limericks about your home town, new hairstyle or disastrous first date… and share them with a fellow laugher.
"There once was a … "

Answering the telephone.

Get cheeky with your manner when picking up the phone: try out different voices, accents and answering messages, have fun with telecommunication!

Laughter slogan.

Have a phrase or slogan up your
sleeve to help with tricky situations
or obvious blunders when they
occur. We need to take ourselves
lightly so have one ready, such as
"Oh that went swimmingly!" "Hey
hoe!" or "Another brilliant move!"

Animal conversation.

Choose a favourite animal and a subject you want to talk about. Converse in your chosen animal language to your partner or group. Actions are permitted but no words allowed. How fluent are you in "baboon"?

Ask for jokes.

Jokes may not always be funny, but if someone shares their joke with you, then laugh anyway, they will feel delighted. As you laugh with them you will be giving your lungs a great work out and ridding your body of stale air and toxins. You can both share jokes and then laugh like they are the best ones you have ever heard.

Make a laughter tape.

Tape-record your family or friends
laughing. Play it back to them
and others and see if you can
guess the laughers. Listening
to laughter is wonderful and the
tape recording will be a treasured
memory for years to come.

Make-believe conversation.

Have a pretend conversation on the telephone or your mobile and get all your friends guessing as to what is going on. You could be on the phone to the BBC or your favourite idol. Use your imagination and have some fun.

Learn a joke.

Joke telling needs some practising. Try to learn about 3 jokes (not too long!) that are aimed at different age groups so that you can use them with different generations. Even if people may not laugh, they will appreciate your efforts to entertain.

Keep funny quotes.

When you read or find a humorous joke, article or video clip, make a note of it to use and share at a later date. Focusing on laughter, comedy and the lighter side of life can give you unexpected inner strength even in challenging circumstances.

Create a comedy script.

If you have a worry or problem at the moment and would like to gain a new perspective, write an imaginary script in your head for your favourite comedian to portray your problem in a humorous light. Include imaginative props, characters and outrageous exaggeration if necessary to make it as funny as possible.

Counting circle.

Have everyone standing close to each other in a circle, then try and count in sequence from 1 up to as many people as there are in the circle, but only one person can say a number at one time. If two people talk at once you have to begin again from 1. This is much harder than it sounds and encourages lots of laughter.

Think positive thoughts.

Smile when you wake up and spend a minute or two thinking happy thoughts. Setting our intentions for the day ahead can be very powerful. What would you like to have happen today?

Make up nonsense words.

Create your own inventive words for specific objects or situations, e.g. "I'm off to *pootle* around the shops."

Physical
moves ...

Ridiculous walks.

Experiment with different imaginative walks down the corridor or to the shops. Walk like you are John Wayne, or as if you are walking on hot sand, or pacing the deck on board a ship in a gale force wind.

Playful waves.

Watch how young children wave to others and copy them. Can you do a double windscreen wiper wave, a royal wave, a shy wave or a helicopter wave? Make up your own wave greetings and try them out when you meet people you know.

Skipping.

Either with or without a rope, this out-dated way of travelling does wonders for raising spirits. Hold skipping competitions. Can you still skip wearing a pinstriped suit or balancing a banana on your head?

Potato and spoon competition.

Play a potato and spoon partner game where you both put one hand behind your back and try to knock your opponent's potato off their spoon with yours. You can make up your own rules. *Warning:* Don't try this with mashed potato!

Body wrestling.

Have an arm wrestle or a finger wrestle. Body wrestling can be fast and furious and can help decide who gets to cook dinner.

Tricks with faces.

Ask others what tricks or party pieces they can do with their faces: ear waggling, eyebrow dancing, eye rolling, gurning … all wonderful talents that encourage laughter and silliness. Can you do them all at the same time?

Slapsies.

Play 'Slapsies' with a willing participant. Place your own hands together with palms touching. Facing your opponent with a cheeky grin, touch your opponent's fingertips gently with your fingertips and wait. On an agreed signal, try to slap your partner's hands quickly before they can take them away. Alternatively they can try to beat you to it and slap yours first. You can make up your own rules.

Laughing on wheels.

Borrow some scooters or rollerblades and set up races and obstacle courses to negotiate. Anything with wheels will do: skateboards, go-carts and tricycles all count. Create your own Grand Prix.

Clapping games.

Invent a clapping game with one or several friends where you try to keep a chant going with a clapping rhythm. This is reminiscent of playground chants and clapping games from years gone by, and surprisingly fun, especially when it all starts to go wrong.

Bottom wiggling.

Hold a bottom wiggling
competition, preferably to
loud music and cheerful
encouragement from others. This
can be executed as a dance or a
walk, depending on the amount of
available space.

Pillow fight.

An oldie but still a goodie. This can also work with cushions, beanbags, even duvets!

Hand jiving.

Play some groovy music and hand jive with a partner to the beat. This is managed easily sitting at a desk or on a train. Extra points given for style and interpretation.

Pants on your head.

This game entails running around in a senseless fashion with a pair of pants and socks; one sock dangling from each ear and a pair of underpants lodged firmly on your head. Try it – it has a surprising effect.

Play 'IT'.

Even with a limited amount of space this is always a favourite, and can be changed to 'Stuck in the mud' to add variety. Laughter occurs naturally when you chase and move your body playfully, just as you did as a child. To keep everyone moving, you can all become 'IT' at the same time.

Games session.

Instead of having a chat or working through lunch, plan a few games in your break with a group of friends. This is an energising way to liven up your lunch hour and will help you work more productively in the afternoon. Try tiddlywinks, card games, or invent some games of your own.

Catching leaves.

Stand under a tree in the autumn and see if you can catch a leaf. This is harder than it sounds. (Acorns are even trickier). When you have succeeded, have a massive leaf throwing fight and encourage others to join in.

Horse racing.

During your break have an imaginary horse race on pretend ponies, racehorses or donkeys to the end of the office corridor and back. This takes imagination but is hysterical to watch. Include hurdles and jumps for your steeds but try not to fall off.

Play snap.

Challenge someone to a game of snap. It feels very childish, very competitive and creates lots of laughter. Luckily, we can revert to a younger mind set whenever we choose to!

Sword fight.

Choose your weapons… cheese straw, chopsticks, plastic spoons… and place them on the desk in front of you facing your opponent. On an agreed signal, pick up your sword and fence as if you were Zorro.

Bounce on a trampoline.

If you are physically able to, try bouncing unrestrainedly on a trampoline, bed or mattress, either on your own or with friends and family. Bodies love to bounce!

Tickle monster.

One of you turns in to a 'Tickle
Monster' and chases the others
around ('home' identified first if
needed). You don't even need to
tickle for the laughs to ensue - the
mere expectation of being tickled
is often enough.

Jogger's laugh.

Not all of us are natural joggers,
but we can use a jogger's warm up
to get the laughter flowing. Start
by breathing deeply and smiling.
Start to walk, (either on the spot or
moving forwards) swinging your
arms and saying 'ha' in rhythm.
Speed up to a jog, then finally a
sprint as you head for the finishing
line, releasing laughter along the
way!

Paddling laugh.

Even in winter this invigorates the body, improves circulation and energises the spirit. Get your wellies at the ready, throw caution to the wind and jump in with both feet.

Windmill laughter.

Start by gently swinging your arms and chuckling slowly. Gradually build momentum at your own pace, swinging your arms with more energy as your laughter builds. Continue until you swing your arms right round in a circle like a windmill, releasing more laughter. (Not suitable for crowded tube journeys.)

Dancing laughter.

Try your hand at hip hop, salsa, waltzing, disco, any type of dancing you fancy. The more you exaggerate the moves the more laughter emerges. Laughing is the 'dancing breath' so with a distinct lack of seriousness, dancing and laughter can make a powerful combination.

Learn Laughter Yoga.

This method of bringing laughter to the body via playful laughter exercises and yogic breathing was devised by Dr Madan Kataria in India in 1995 and is now a worldwide movement. There are many communities and laughter clubs practising laughter yoga. It can be adapted to all regardless of age or physical fitness.
Go to www.laughteryoga.org for more details.

Housework laughter.

Make up your own variety of laughs to accompany the different household chores you do. If you have to do them, they may as well be fun. Try a 'lawnmower laugh', a 'dare-devil dusting laugh' or a 'spring-clean chuckle'.

Making and creating ...

Playdoh.

Make imaginative sculptures out of clay, playdoh or plasticine. No-one is ever too old for the squashy stuff.

Creative chalk.

Chalk a cheerful picture on the pavement to encourage people to smile. Leave the chalk nearby with an arrow pointing to the picture so that each person who comes along can add their cartoon, picture or smiley face.

Funny handshake.

Make up a funny handshake with a mate or member of your family... include sounds, swivels, high fives, chants, anything goes and make it enthusiastic. Practice it often and then use it each time you greet them.

Celebrity laughter.

Choose a famous celebrity and laugh like her or him, the more outrageous the better. See if others can guess which one you are demonstrating.

Self-portrait.

Draw self-portraits with a difference. The caller calls out different parts of the anatomy in turn and the drawers must draw each part freely with their eyes shut. The end results can be framed or pinned up and shared. It is great if they can be signed by the artist, (using their other hand to sign the signature).

Arranging fruit.

Instead of arranging flowers, give a little artistry to your vegetables or fruit collection by creating pictures, patterns or rude sculptures. Display your art for all to see.

Balloon art.

Draw silly faces or comical images on blown up balloons and then release them. If you have any frustrating problems this is useful for releasing tension; you can write or draw the issues on the balloons and watch them disappear as you release the balloon into the sky.

Finger faces.

Draw characters on your fingers and make them talk, dance and interact with each other. Create scenery, costumes and props as appropriate. Let your imagination and fingers go wild.

Laughter bubble.

As you smile, imagine a bubble
of unconditional love surrounding
you. Your bubble will have its own
unique colour and texture. Stay in
the bubble as long as you want.
Try laughing into your bubble and
seeing what happens, does it
change colour or shape?

Use visual reminders.

When you text friends or family or emailing, use 'smileys' or fun visual additions to your message. The person who receives it will know you are smiling and wishing them well.

Laughter face paint

Decorate your face with symbols
and colours that signify laughter.
Make your face as joyful as
possible and dress up in colourful
clothes to match.

Singing, dancing and laughing ...

Sing your heart out.

Make a list of fun songs, put them in a hat and pull out one at random to sing operatic style, country and western style, or whatever style comes to mind.

Terrible singing.

Hold a truly tuneless singing
competition where people have
to sing their very WORST. Anyone
singing remotely in tune gets
thrown out of the running. Prize for
the most talented tuneless singer.

Musical laughter.

Some musicals are full of joyful songs that truly lift our spirits. Watch favourite musicals with friends or family. Sing along and dance with gusto!

Singing laughter.

Gather a group of friends or colleagues together and try out some laughter sounds to get your laughing tonsils warmed up. Then sing a famous song like "Bear Necessities" and use laughter sounds to put laughter to music.

Birthday serenade.

When it is someone's birthday,
treat them to a loving serenade
such as 'You're the one that I want'
(Grease) with the whole family or
office singing to them. Have some
singers on bended knee and
others on percussion. Additions
such as a single carnation in the
teeth or a proffered chocolate
éclair are nice touches.

Business meeting rap.

Start or conclude a meeting by commenting on progress in a 'rap' style, bling optional.

Operatic greeting.

Meet with a group of friends, sing hello and greet each other in operatic style, huge arm gestures included.

Jamming session.

Hold a 'jamming' session in the office, staffroom or at home with everyday objects. Donate a prize for the most imaginative instrument. Work out a rap, a rhythm or find a familiar tune to follow.

Daring dancing.

Try out some zany moves in the kitchen, living room, bus shelter… be Tina Turner, John Travolta, a demented ballerina… let your imagination go wild. This is great for embarrassing the children.

Tap dance laughter

Tap your toes and laugh at the same time to an upbeat song of your choice. This can be performed sitting or standing. Add arm movements if you can for some real tap dancing flair.

Laughter chant.

One person leads others in a short rousing chant, e.g. "We're the laughers loud and proud." (Others repeat this.) "Join us in this one big crowd..." (Others repeat.)

Create a laughter environment ...

Cartoon strips.

Find and cut out favourite cartoons
from newspapers, magazines and
leaflets to display on the walls.
Funny cards received are worth
collecting and displaying too.

Wear outrageous clothes.

Experiment with wearing a silly
tie, wig, hat or brooch at a jaunty
angle. See how you feel and notice
how your accessory affects others
around you. Play with colours
and patterns and begin to collect
clothes that make you feel bright
and cheerful.

Laughter mascot.

Adopt a laughter mascot at work or home. Place it in various positions to make yourself smile and to surprise fellow colleagues or family members.

Laughter toys.

Collect silly toys and ridiculous objects that remind you of laughter and put them in your workplace, car or shed to remind you to lighten up.

Laughter alarm.

Set an alarm in your kitchen or on your office computer to go off regularly throughout the day to remind you to have fun and giggle. Buy a cheeky or amusing alarm clock that will act as a visual reminder to lighten your mood.

Laughter space.

Find a space in your room, shed, office or kitchen that knows about laughter and joy. Stand next to the space and look at it from different angles. Does it have a colour, size or texture? What happens when you stand in this space? Try first putting a toe in, then a whole leg, then your whole body.

Laughter posters.

Brighten up your everyday environment with fun, silly and colourful posters and pictures of people laughing. You can make your own montage of funny photos and memories.

Laughter library.

Set up a laughter library at home or work where people can borrow and swap DVD's, books, CD's and laughter toys. Keep adding new objects to it to keep it fresh and well used.

Everyday object laughter.

Collect a number of everyday objects from your desk or kitchen and bring them to life with characters, voices, mannerisms and playfulness. Children are adept at this so ask them for help if you are stuck for ideas. You can get the objects singing, dancing and acting in strange but wonderful ways. Amusing and imaginative stories can unfold.

Laughter book.

Keep your own laughter book with ideas for laughter, jokes you love and funny quotes that have tickled you pink. Keeping this in full view and easily accessible will encourage you and others to use it frequently.

Laughter metaphor:

When you really laugh ... that's like what?

If possible, think of times when you really laugh heartily. What was that like? Once you establish an image or metaphor of what laughter is like for you, draw or paint this image and keep it in full view.

Use a ridiculous pen.

Find a really outrageous pen to write with, the more ridiculous the better.

Mad hair day.

Pick a day to go wild with hair fashion, wear bunches, 'scrunchies' and even hair dye to perfect an outrageously crazy hair affair. Prize for the most vividly different hairstyle from normal.

Laughter hat.

Design your own laughter hat. Find a suitably funky hat, decorate it as you like or simply find one that makes you feel playful. Put the hat on and dance, smile or laugh enthusiastically. Soon you may find yourself 'anchored' to the hat via laughter and will only need to see the hat to start smiling. This can be adapted for laughter glasses, wigs, a fake moustache or accessory that is easy to remove when you want to finish.

Moustache day.

Hire, buy or make a decent size moustache to wear to work, the shops or a friend's house for the evening. Try to act normal.

Shower cap laughter.

Gather a group of friends together, go and see a funny film and all wear shower caps, outrageous wigs or silly hats.

Make your own laughter sign.

Create your own sign or quote about laughter or joy and hang it in a prominent place where you will see it frequently.

Playful
connections ...

Laughter echoes.

Set up a round of laughter around the office or in teams, where one member of the team starts by offering a hearty laugh, then the others copy it and send it on. At any time the laugh can change in tempo, volume or pitch. Speed the process up. Once you start getting faster with the echo, real laughter will often emerge.

Holding it in laugh.

Tell everyone to take a deep breath in and hold it whilst blowing out their cheeks. They must wait while you count down to zero, and mustn't laugh before you get there. Glare madly at them if they smile or snigger. Slowly, you start to count down from 5 or 6 (lots of eye contact for this one). Great for when you are all sitting in a circle trying to be serious.

Play 'rock, paper, and scissors'.

Use this age-old challenge with a partner to decide who makes the tea. You can also invent your own version of the game and add sound-effects. Try 'giants, wizards and knights' or 'eagles, owls and mice'. Decide who wins and why.

Whoopee cushion.

Buy or borrow a whoopee cushion.
Need we say more?

Paper fight.

Collect all the unwanted or damaged paper at the end of the day before re-cycling it. Divide the paper pile into two different piles, one for each team. On a given word, both teams grab a piece of paper, scrunch it and throw at the other team. After two minutes the winner is the team that has the most paper balls on their opponent's side of the room.

Mini holiday.

Think of 5 things you would normally do on holiday and bring them into the day for some adventurous creativity. Tasting different foods, listening to another language, lying in a hammock, visiting a museum, going snorkelling… all possible with a bit of forward planning.

Three-legged race.

Find a willing partner in crime and attach your limbs together, race to the end of the corridor, car park or field. No health and safety in this one, so beware!

Mustn't laugh.

Challenge your friend, colleague or neighbour to a 'mustn't laugh or smile' competition. You can do or say anything to make each other laugh or smile, but you mustn't smile or laugh yourself. This is very hard!

Winking.

This is almost a lost art. Wink very cheekily at friends and family and notice what reaction you get.

Hugging laughter.

When meeting up with a favourite friend or family member, hold them in a warm embrace. Start laughing as you give them a gorgeous hug. Hugging laughter is highly contagious due to the close contact.

Clapping laughter.

Devise a clapping rhythm with a partner that you can do together facing each other. Get faster and faster...

Feeling and laughing ...

Crying laughter.

If you feel like crying then pretend to cry. Exhibit large exaggerated sobs and wails. This often turns to laughter but if it turns to crying that's all healthy too... it will release a lot of pent up emotion and sometimes we need to cry before we can laugh.

Funniest memory.

What is the funniest thought, memory or picture you could think right now? Turn up the colour and brightness of the picture, bring it closer and imagine yourself stepping into the picture to experience it all as vividly as possible.

Tree laughter.

This is a fabulous way to release tension and the stresses of the day. Find a willing fellow laugher or two and head for the park or grassy field. Find a leafy tree, lie down, get comfy, then look up through the branches and laugh together. Make sure there are no pigeons above you.

Mad professor.

When you are feeling miserable, tired or annoyed, play with the feeling by exaggerating it wildly. Make noises, wail and gnash your teeth if necessary to acknowledge the feeling and then let it go. You could end up laughing at yourself along the way.

Exaggeration.

When faced by a tricky problem or stressful situation, exaggerate the situation to the ridiculous. This may help you see the problem from a lighter perspective.

Showering with laughter.

Singing in the shower is great for the lungs, and so is laughing. Give yourself permission to really let go and laugh as you shampoo, scrub and clean between your toes. No-one is likely to hear you and you can experiment with the different laughter sounds. Works really well with freezing cold showers!

Laughter pill.

Call in a 'Laughter Doctor' who administers laughter pills. They are easy to swallow and take effect slowly but surely to ensure the giggles spread throughout your body. The giggle effect starts from your toes and works its way up to your mouth, head and arms… the effect can take a while to subside.

Find a laughter expert.

When in the company of a child or a young pet, notice and copy how they play. Lower yourself to their level on the floor and get into their games with them. See how it feels to move like them, breathe like them and be them for a day as closely as you can. Use detective methods to find out how they manage to be so playful and 'in the moment'; they have so much to teach us.

Tantrum laughter.

When life isn't going your way and you are feeling frustrated or mad about something, start stamping your feet. Scream blue murder or wave your arms about. Lie down on the floor and tantrum if you want to. Feeling silly and foolish is one of the quickest pathways to laughter.

Superhero laughter.

Wear your pants on the outside of your clothes and be a superhero for the day. You could be 'Custard Man', 'Reptile Woman', or 'Captain Crudité'...

Laughing on the inside.

When you really can't laugh…
when you are in pain or it hurts to
laugh…imagine you are laughing
silently inside. This will release
endorphins to help reduce the pain
and help you to smile.

Laughter experiment.

Walk up to someone, explain that you are carrying out some research on laughter and ask them to try out various laughs with you. Encourage them to be adventurous and join in laughing with them.

Laughing out loud.

When laughing, experiment with opening your mouth a tiny bit wider than normal and see what happens.

Laughing at life.

Take turns with a group of
supportive friends to laugh at
the everyday frustrations of life.
Simply stand up and say your
name, then laugh. Next, share an
annoying happening in your life
currently that is causing you a
bit of bother and then laugh. Ask
everyone to laugh with you on cue,
encouraging you to take the lighter
view of the situation. If this is
done repetitively then the laughter
usually gathers momentum,
releasing built up stress in its path.

Traffic light laughter.

Every time you stop at a red light try a gentle chuckle. This can become a regular laughter reminder and might help you to relax while you wait.

Wild and wacky laughter ...

Laughter cushion.

Taking an ordinary cushion, explain to your friends or family that the cushion has secret laughter powers and that every time it is raised in the air, laughter appears. Test it out with a short laugh, check everyone is with you, and then take turns passing the cushion around to get laughs from the group.

Driving laughter.

When you are driving along see how many miles you can do when chuckling or laughing. (Nobody knows you are not listening to the radio.) Think of a funny incident or merely bring laughter to your body playfully using some of the laughter sounds: Ha, Ho, Hu, Hee, or Hoo. This is a good way to spend time in traffic jams.

Copy people who laugh easily.

Start noticing the people around you who laugh easily or people who are generally playful and watch their body language. What are they doing that helps them laugh freely? Do they throw their head back, take deep breaths or keep eye contact? Keep curious about laughter. Particularly notice how small children laugh; they are the natural experts on playing and laughing.

Surround yourself with laughers.

Find people who enjoy laughing for its own sake and hang out with them as much as you can. People who love to laugh are often playful in nature and up for a good time. They don't mind taking risks and are often very sociable. Meet regularly with these friends and take turns in suggesting novel ideas to keep things fun.

Cheering competition.

In the office, at the football ground or at the bus stop have a cheering competition. This really exercises the fun muscles and the lungs at the same time. Cheering is great for the soul and is incredibly energising. If it's someone's birthday give them 3 cheers, or if even because someone made the tea that day. Even the smallest things in life are worth a cheer. Cheer just because it's Wednesday!

Coat striptease.

Possible best done in winter when we wear loads of layers. When arriving at the office, a meeting or a friend's house, sing or hum the striptease song as you unravel your coat, umbrella, scarf, bag, sunglasses etc. (You don't have to strip off everything!)

Clowning around.

Book yourself a clowning workshop or comedy improvisation course to really tickle your funny bone and encourage the playful side of you.

Tickly clothes.

Imagine as you get dressed that your clothes are tickling you madly. Fidget, wriggle and giggle as you get dressed or undressed. This is a great way of encouraging young children to get dressed and provides additional warmth on a cold winter morning.

Laughter master.

Pretend you are a big laugher for a day. Even if you don't feel like it yet, acting 'as if' you were a confident laugher could give useful insights into how to laugh freely and easily.

Regression laughter.

For the next five minutes, pretend you are 5 years old again, or whatever age for you could be very playful. What could you be doing, seeing or feeling?

Comedy night for beginners.

Encourage others to come along with their favourite jokes, games, dressing up clothes, wigs or false noses and have a night swapping funny stories, songs, jokes and poems.

Lick your elbow.

Challenge others around you to lick their own elbows, touch their nose with their tongue or make a noise with their armpit. Invent a playful challenge that will help make you and your friends look ridiculous and enable you all to take yourselves lightly. This passes the time in long queues and gets everyone involved.

Water fight laughter.

Using cups, bowls or other household objects, start a neighbourhood water fight in the garden or outside space. Laughter pretty much guaranteed.

Group
laughter ...

Themed nights out.

Plan fun nights out regularly with a group of like-minded, fun friends who love to laugh. Create themes for the evenings or try out new venues to keep it playful. Laughing in a group is highly contagious.

Sardines.

One person is chosen to hide. The others go and look for him or her and when they find the hidden person they quietly hide with them. Best played in the dark, this game is very childish and totally silly, great for initiating laughter.

Hide and seek.

Play good old fashioned 'hide and seek' at home, in the office or in a supermarket. The winner gets a prize. Hone your skills of stealth to avoid capture.

Jelly throwing.

Everyone bring dirty overalls, painting shirts or old tatty clothes and hold a jelly throwing contest after work or in the park. Call all your friends or colleagues and really go for it. Messy but fun.

Rugby pass laughter.

Form a circle and pass an imaginary rugby ball round the circle, grunting 'ho' as you quickly pass the ball from person to person. Say 'ha' each time you change direction round the circle. When you want to score a try, raise the ball high in the air and everyone has to cheer. To initiate a scrum, someone shouts 'scrum' and you all link arms, kicking your legs frantically. A quick warm-up game to bond people and to energise small groups.

Synchronised swimming.

Form teams to attempt 'synchronised swimming' as if entering for the Olympics. Have a judge who calls out commands such as 'front crawl', 'backstroke' or 'freestyle' and gives points for enthusiasm and timing. This has to be seen to be believed and is a great warm up for a meeting or team talk.

Lying down laughter.

Lie down on the floor with some like-minded fun people and begin to laugh. Even pretending to laugh at first will encourage free laughter and sooner or later the laughter will turn genuine and burst forth spontaneously and unrestrainedly. Allow the laughter to stay as long as it wants, or as long as you can stand. This can be a great release and is highly contagious. Finish with some slow deep breathing to relax and calm body and mind.

Head on belly laughter.

Do 'Lying down laughter' with a group of people who know each other well. Lay on your back with your head on your friend's tummy. Then another person in the group lies on their back with their head on your tummy and so on. Let the laughter flow and the tummies bounce!

Infectious laughter.

Pretend that you are starting a laughter infection in the office, bus or pub and get everyone in on the act. Start laughing in gentle sniggers and then get people to join in at different stages in their own style. Offer some exaggerated laughs, some timid, some shy, some wild and expressive, but all adding to the contagiousness.

Group sculpture.

In groups, create a group sculpture together to depict a single place, object or animal. The other groups can try to guess what it is.

Join a laughter club.

Find out where your nearest laughter club is. If there isn't a club in your area, find out how to set one up. Laughing in a group is highly contagious and a great way of connecting with others in your community or workplace. There are many laughter clubs around the UK, which are listed on www.laughternetwork.co.uk .

Enjoy
laughing ...

Visit the zoo.

Find the most playful animal and watch to see how it communicates, moves and enjoys life. Young animals spend a great deal of time playing as it is essential to their development, just as it is for ours. Can you imitate a meerkat, a monkey or even a mammoth?

Re-live funny moments.

At the end of the day, re-run in your mind a video of funny things that have happened, exaggerating wildly where necessary. You can add artistic direction to your video, so add music, commentary, props, cartoon voices, anything that helps you to smile and enjoy the day's humour before you go to sleep.

Enjoy your own unique sense of humour.

Indulge in your favourite comedy re-runs, videos, radio shows and clips on the internet. Remind yourself on a regular basis what tickles your funny bone and enjoy it as regularly as possible.

Laughter clicker.

Use a clicker (similar to those used for training puppies) to record how many times you laugh in one day. You may be surprised at how much or how little you laugh currently.

Guess the laugher.

Gather a group of people together and blindfold one person. Take it in turns to giggle while they have to guess who the laugher is. You could try a 'mad professor' laugh, a pirate laugh or even a 'hyena' laugh to try to foil them.

Celebration laughter.

Celebrate good news, however small, by smiling and laughing if you can. Use any excuse to exercise your facial muscles and lungs. Take five minutes at the end of every day to look back and remember fond moments.

Just laugh.

There doesn't have to be a reason or a special moment for laughter. Contrary to popular belief, you don't need an external joke or situation to make you laugh. If you are willing, then you can choose to laugh anytime, anywhere. When you feel like it, start gently with a smile, then a chuckle, and see what happens. Laughter is totally free and portable!

Laugh on your own.

Laugh daily on your own. Discover what helps you to laugh freely and laugh by yourself as often as possible. Love your laughter – it expresses who you really are.

Enjoy laughing!

Indulge in a hearty laugh whenever possible, both on your own and with others. Laughing is fantastic for our health, lighter fuel for the spirit and too good to leave to chance.

Lift life with laughter!

www.laughterlinescoaching.co.uk

We provide a range of services:

★ Laughter training

★ Laughter talks for conferences

★ Laughter workshops for businesses and organisations

★ Coaching and mentoring

★ A monthly laughter club based in Chichester, West Sussex, UK

www.laughterlinescoaching.co.uk

La**O**ghterlines COACHING

Please connect with us by:

★ Visiting our website at
  www.laughterlinescoaching.co.uk

★ Joining our Laughterlines Coaching
  page on Facebook

★ Following us on twitter
  @lisa_sturge

★ Emailing
  lisa@laughterlinescoaching.co.uk
  with your laughter stories and ideas.

We would love to hear from you!

This page is for your own laughter ideas and notes...

About the Author

Lisa Sturge founded Laughterlines Coaching in 2007 to encourage people to laugh and play more in everyday life. Having trained initially in the educational field as a teacher and special needs co-ordinator, she is now a laughter facilitator, public speaker, trainer and personal development coach. She loves to have adventures and climb trees and never wants to grow up.